THE
UNITED STATES
OF AMERICA
REFERENCE BOOK

by
Orville V. Webster III

I0964967

JBG PUBLISHING
Los Angeles
Printed in the United States
All Rights Reserved

TABLE OF CONTENTS

TABLE OF CONTENTS

IMPORTANT DATES IN UNITED STATES HISTORY

1492 Columbus sights land on October 12 in what is today known as the Bahamas.

1497 John Cabot explores the area extending from Canada to Delaware.

1513 Juan Ponce de Leon explores the coast of Florida.

1524 Giovanni da Verrazon leads a French expedition along the coast between Carolina and Nova Scotia, at one point entering New York harbor.

1579 Francis Drake claims California for Great Britain.

1607 Jamestown, Virginia becomes the first European settlement in America.

1609 Henry Hudson explores the Hudson River and New York harbor.

1619 The firt black slaves are landed by the Dutch at Jamestown, Virginia.

1620 The Pilgrims land in Plymouth, Massachusetts. The Mayflower Compact is drafted and signed later that year.

1623 New Netherland (later New York) is founded by the Dutch.

1626 Manhattan Island is sold to Peter Minuit by the Indians for trinkets valued at twenty-four dollars.

1634 Maryland is founded as a Catholic colony with religious tolerance.

1635 New Hampshire is founded by Captain John Mason.

1636 Harvard is founded, becoming the first college in America.

1663 New Jersey is founded by Sir George Cateret and Sir William Berekely. The Carolinas are founded later that year.

1664 Three hundred English soldiers capture New Netherland from the Dutch.

1683 Pennsylvania is founded by William Penn.

1692 19 persons are executed in the Witchcraft trials in Salem, Massachusetts.

1712 21 black persons are executed after slaves revolt in New York.

1732 Georgia is founded.

1752 Benjamin Franklin proves that lightning is electricity while flying a kite during a thunderstorm.

1754 The French and Indian—or Seven Year—War begins.

1758 The first Indian reservation is established.

1763 The French and Indian—or Seven Year—War ends.

1765 Nine colonies sign the Declaration of Rights after Britain passes the Stamp Act.

1766 Great Britain repeals the Stamp Act.

1767 The passage of the Townshend Acts institutes taxes on glass, paper, painter's lead, and tea.

1770 British troops kill five colonists in the Boston Massacre.

1773 The Boston Tea Party occurs.

1775 Patrick Henry gives his "Give me liberty or give me death" speech in front of the Virginia convention. Paul Revere and William Dawes ride to alert patriots of that the "British are coming." The battles of Lexington and Concord signal the beginning of the American Revolution. The battle of Bunker Hill occurs.

1776 The Declaration of Independence is drafted and signed.

1777 Washington defeats Lord Cornwallis at Princeton; the Continental Congress adopts the Stars and Stripes. Declaration of Independence approved.

1778 France sends a fleet to assist the United States.

1781 British defeated at Yorktown by Colonial and French armies.

1783 Britain, United States, sign treaty ending the Revolutionary War.

1787 The Constitutional Convention opens in Philadelphia.

1788 New Hampshire's ratification of the Constitution places it into effect.

1789 George Washington becomes the first President; John Adams, Vice President; Thomas Jefferson, Secretary of State; Alexander Hamilton, Secretary of Treasury.

1790 Congress votes to establish a new capital along the Potomac River.

1791 The Bill of Rights goes into effect.

1793 Eli Whitney invents the cotton gin, thus reviving slavery in the South.

1796 Washington gives his farewell address.

1803 The United States doubles its land holdings with the purchase of the Louisiana Territory from Napoleon.

1804 Vice President Aaron Burr kills Alexander Hamilton in a duel.

1812 The War of 1812 begins.

1814 The Treaty of Ghent signals the end of the War of 1812. Francis Scott Key writes the words to the "Star Spangled Banner."

1823 The Monroe Doctrine enunciated.

1825 The opening of the Erie Canal cuts travel time from Buffalo to New York City by one-third.

1831 Nat Turner leads a slave rebellion in Virginia; he is later captured, tried, and hanged.

1836 Texans are besieged at San Antonio's Alamo by Mexicans under Santa Anna. Texas later declares its independence from Mexico.

1838 The Cherokee Indians begin the Trail of Tears, a 1,200 mile mandatory journey to Oklahoma.

1844 Samuel F. B. Morse sends the first message via telegraph from Washington to Baltimore. It reads: "What hath God wrought!"

1846 War is declared by the United States on Mexico. The U.S. will subsequently receive Arizona, California, New Mexico, Nevada, Texas, Utah, and a portion of Colorado as a result of a treaty signed with their neighbors to the south. Another treaty with Britain awards the U.S. the Oregon Territory to the 49th parallel (Hence the slogan, "54 40 or fight").

1848 Gold is discovered in California.

1857 The Supreme Court's Dred Scott decision upholds slavery.

1860 Abraham Lincoln elected president.

1861 Confederates defeat Union troops at the Battle of Bull Run.

1862 Homestead Act approved.

1863 Harriet Tubman frees 750 slaves. President Lincoln gives the Gettysburg Address and issued the Emancipation Proclamation, freeing "all slaves in areas still in rebellion."

1864 General Sherman captures Atlanta.

1865 The Civil War ends when the Confederacy surrenders at Appomattox, Virginia. President Lincoln assassinated by John Wilkes Booth. The Thirteenth Amendment abolishes slavery.

1869 Transcontinental railroad completed.

1876 General Custer goes down to defeat at the Battle of Little Bighorn.

1881 President Garfield is shot; he dies later that year. Sitting Bull surrenders. Tuskegee Institute founded by Booker T. Washington.

1890 Police kill Sitting Bull at Standing Rock Reservation, South Dakota. Sioux Indians are massacred by soldiers at Wounded Knee, South Dakota, the last major battle between Indians and U.S. troops.

1898 The United States declares war on Spain; troops invade Puerto Rico and liberate it from Spain.

1901 President McKinley assassinated by Leon Czolgosz.

1903 Panama signs the Panama Canal treaty. First automobile trip across the country taken from San Francisco to New York. The Wright brothers make their first flights in a mechanically propelled airplane.

1906 The San Francisco earthquake and fire kills 503 people.

1915 First conversation via telephone occurs, from New York to San Francisco, between Alexander Graham Bell and Thomas A. Watson.

1917 The United States declares war on Germany.

1918 World War I ends.

1920 The Eighteenth Amendment bans the sale of alcohol. Sacco and Vanzetti found guilty and executed for murder. The Nineteenth Amendment gives women the right to vote.

1925 John T. Scopes is found guilty of teaching the theory of evolution in a Dayton, Tennessee high school.

1927 Charles Lindbergh flies the Spirit of St. Louis from New York to Paris, marking the first intercontinental flight.

1929 "St. Valentine's Day Massacre" occurs in Chicago. Teapot Dome scandal rocks the government. The stock market crash signals the beginning of the Great Depression.

1933 During the "100 days" special session, Congress passes New Deal social and economic reforms. Prohibition ends with passage of 21st amendment.

1935 The Social Security Act is passed.

1941 Japan bombs Pearl Harbor, bringing the U.S. into World War II.

1944 U.S. Allied forces stage the D-Day invasion of Normandy.

1945 The Yalta conference brings Russian into World War II against Japan. President Roosevelt dies, Truman takes over. World War II ends as Germany and Japan are defeated. U.S. forces liberate Dachau concentration camp. The U.S. drops atomic bombs on Hiroshima and Nagasaki.

1947 The Marshall plan for European aid is announced. Jackie Robinson breaks baseball's color barrier.

1949 NATO formed by the U.S., Canada and ten European nations.

1950 U.S. sends military advisors to South Vietnam.

1951 The Rosenbergs are found guilty and sentenced to death for espionage.

1954 The Supreme Court's *Brown v. Board of Education* ruling outlaws segregation in public schools.

1955 Rosa Parks refuses to give up her seat in a bus to a white person, beginning the Montgomery, Alabama bus boycott.

1958 The first U.S. satellite, Explorer I, is launched into orbit.

1959 Alaska and Hawaii become the 49th and 50th states.

1960 Over 70,000 black and white students participate in sit-ins to protest an incident that saw four blacks be refused service at a lunch counter in Greensboro, North Carolina.

1961 The invasion of Cuba's "Bay of Pigs" by U.S.-backed Cuban exiles is thwarted. Alan B. Shepard, Jr. travels on the first U.S. manned sub-orbital space flight.

1962 President Kennedy orders the blockade of Cuba, thus setting off the Cuban Missile Crisis. John H. Glenn, Jr. becomes the first American in orbit.

1963 Martin Luther King, Jr. heads a civil rights march in Washington D.C. President John F. Kennedy assassinated in Dallas.

1965 Malcolm X is assassinated. Martin Luther King, Jr. heads a march in Selma, Alabama.

1967 200,000 people march in New York City in protest of the Vietnam War.

1968 500 Vietnamese are massacred by U.S. troops in the My Lai incident. Communist troops attack Saigon during the "Tet Offensive." Martin Luther King, Jr. is assassinated. Robert F. Kennedy is assassinated.

1969 300,000 go to Woodstock, New York for "three days of peace and music." Sen. Edward Kennedy involved in Chappaquiddick incident. Astronaut Neil Armstrong becomes the first man to set foot on the moon.

1970 The Ohio National Guard kills four Kent State University students protesting the Vietnam war. 18 year olds given the right to vote.

1972 Governor George Wallace is shot and seriously wounded. President Nixon visits China. The Watergate break-in occurs.

1973 The Supreme Court rules that states can't prevent a woman from having an abortion during the initial six months of pregnancy. Watergate hearings occur. Vice President Spiro T. Agnew resigns.

1974 President Nixon resigns.

1979 A major accident occurs at the Three Mile Island nuclear power plant. Iranian students take 63 Americans hostage at the U.S. embassy in Tehran.

1980 Ronald Reagan elected president. John Lennon murdered by Mark David Chapman.

1981 Iran releases 52 American hostages who had been held for 444 days. President Reagan survives an assassination attempt. The Senate confirms the appointment of Sandra Day O'Connor, the first woman ever appointed to the Supreme Court.

1985 President Reagan and General Secretary of the Soviet Communist Party Gorbachev hold a summit conference in Geneva, Switzerland.

1986 The space shuttle Challenger explodes, killing all 6 astronauts and civilian Christa McAuliffe. U.S. officials predict that AIDS cases and deaths will increase tenfold during the next five years.

1987 The Senate and House committees investigate the Iran-Contra affair.

1988 George Bush elected President of the United States.

1989 A powerful earthquake rocks Northern California, killing 59 people and forcing the postponement of the World Series.

BIOGRAPHIES
OF THE
41 PRESIDENTS
OF THE
UNITED STATES

GEORGE WASHINGTON (1789-1797)

Our nation's first president was born on February 22, 1932 (February 11, 1731, old style). Working as a land surveyor in is early years, Washington inherited his half-brother Lawrence's land in 1752—over 100,000 acres in all.

After a fairly successful military career, which included the taking of Ford Duquesne from the French in 1758, Washington was made commander-in-chief by the Continental Congress on June 15, 1775. This was followed by a stint as the chairman of the Constitutional Convention of 1787, where he helped ratify the Constitution, and was eventually elected President and inaugurated on April 30, 1789.

While he was reelected in 1792, Washington refused to accept a third term, and in 1796 he retired to Mount Vernon, where he died on December 14, 1799 after suffering acute laryngitis, contracted from a horse ride in foul weather.

JOHN ADAMS (1797-1801)

Born in Braintree (Quincy), Massachuessetts on October 30, 1735 (October 19, o.s.), John Adams was a Harvard-educated lawyer. He was well known for having argued against taxation without representation before the royal governor in 1765. In 1770, he defended the British soldiers who participated in the "Boston Massacre."

After a stint as George Washington's vice president, he took over the executive office in 1796. He died the same day as Thomas Jefferson—July 4, 1826, exactly 50 years after they had helped adopt the Declaration of Independence.

THOMAS JEFFERSON (1801-1809)

When Thomas Jefferson was 14 years old, his father died, leaving him 2,750 acres of land and all of the slaves that he owned. Jefferson, born April 13, 1743 (April 2, o.s.), studied the classics at the College of William and Mary.

After writing the first draft of the Declaration of Independence, Jefferson was elected governor of Virginia in 1779. He resigned in 1781, worked as the minister to France, and was appointed secretary of state by George Washington in 1789. He lost the presidential election of 1796 to John Adams, but took over the office of vice president.

In 1800, Jefferson tied Aaron Burr in the voting for president, but was appointed the office by a vote in the House of Representatives. The Louisiana Purchase of 1803, and the Lewis and Clark expedition of 1803-1806 were two highlights of his presidential career. He died on July 4, 1826, the same day as John Adams and the 50th anniversary of the adoption of the Declaration of Independence.

JAMES MADISON (1809-1817)

The 4th president of the U.S. was born on March 16, 1751 (March 5, 1750, o.s.), was a member of the Continental Congress, and was elected to the House of Representatives in 1789, where he helped draw up the Bill of Rights. Thomas Jefferson appointed him as secretary of state in 1801.

Madison was elected president in 1808, and he held the office for two terms until 1817, when he retired to his estate at Montpelier. During his presidency, the nation endured the War of 1812. He died on June 28, 1836.

JAMES MONROE (1817-1825)

Educated at the College of William and Mary, James Monroe held a variety of top positions, including U.S. senator (1790), minister to France (1794-96), governor of Virginia (1799-1802), negotiator during the Louisiana Purchase, and secretary of state for James Madison (1811-1817).

Monroe, born April 28, 1758, was elected president in 1816, and reelected by a landslide in 1820. The highlight of his presidential career was undoubtedly the "Monroe Doctrine," a landmark document of foreign policy. He died July 4, 1831.

JOHN QUINCY ADAMS (1825-1829)

The son of John Adams, John Quincy served as an American minister throughout Europe, helping to draft the peace treaty for the War of 1812. He was a U.S. senator from 1803-1808, and the secretary of state under President Monroe. After serving as president from 1825-1829, Adams served 17 years in Congress. Born July 11, 1767, he died in the Speaker's Room of the House of Representatives on February 23, 1848.

ANDREW JACKSON (1829-1837)

13 years after his birth on March 15, 1767, Andrew Jackson joined the militia in the Revolution only to be captured by British troops. He went on to have a very successful military career, and became president in 1828 when he defeated the incumbent John Quincy Adams. After a checkered presidency, he died on June 8, 1845.

MARTIN VAN BUREN (1837-1841)

A former U.S. senator, the one-time governor of New York, and the secretary of state under Andrew Jackson, Martin Van Buren was elected president in 1836. An extremely adept politician, he was, however, never able to gain reelection despite repeated attempts. Born on December 5, 1782, he died on July 24, 1862.

WILLIAM HENRY HARRISON (1841)

Born February 8, 1773, William Henry Harrison was the first governor of Indiana Territory, and a successful major general. He was elected to Congress (1816-1819) and the Senate (1825-1828), before gaining the presidency in 1840. Unfortunately, he caught pneumonia during his inauguration ceremony and died on April 4, 1841, after serving only 31 days in office.

JOHN TYLER (1841-1845)

An independent Whig, John Tyler had a varied political career, serving in the House of Delegates (1811), in Congress (1816-1821), as governor of Virginia (1825-1826), and in the U.S. senate (1827-1836). The vice president to William Henry Harrison, he took over after the latter's death. He signed the resolution for the annexation of Texas on March 1, 1845. Born on March 29, 1790, Tyler died on January 18, 1862.

JAMES KNOX POLK (1845-1849)

This one time Congressman and governor of Tennessee was born on November 2, 1795. Polk defeated Henry Clay as a darkhorse candidate in the 1844 presidential election. He is best remembered for triggering the Mexican War, which garnered the United States both California and the entire Southwest.

A hardcore expansionist, he died a few months after leaving office, on June 15, 1849.

ZACHARY TAYLOR (1849-1850)

This brilliant major general had many triumphs during the Mexican War, becoming nothing short of a national hero. Taylor, born November 24, 1784, was elected president in 1848 as a member of the Whig party. He died in office on July 9, 1850.

MILLARD FILMORE (1850-1853)

The man who took over the executive office when President Taylor died had a rocky term and was not reelected. Born January 7, 1800, Filmore was a member of the state assembly (1829-1832) and Congress (1833-1835; 1837-1843) before taking over the vice presidency. He died on March 8, 1874.

FRANKLIN PIERCE (1853-1857)

The 14th president was born on November 23, 1804. A lawyer, congressman (1833-1837), and U.S. senator (1837-1842), he eventually became a brigadier general during the Mexican War. Elected in 1852, he served only one term. Pierce died on October 8, 1869.

JAMES BUCHANAN (1857-1861)

A volunteer in the War of 1812, James Buchanan

was born on April 23, 1791. His long and distinguished political career included stints in Congress (1820-1831) and the Senate (1834-1845), several years as the secretary of state (1845-1849), and some time as the minister to Britain (1853). He defeated John C. Fremont and Millard Fillmore to gain the 1856 presidential election. Once in office, he denied the right of states to secede. Buchanan died on June 1, 1868.

ABRAHAM LINCOLN (1861-1865)

Born in a log cabin on February 12, 1809, Abraham Lincoln went on to become one of our most popular presidents. He began his political career in 1834 as a member of the Illinois General Assembly. He became a lawyer in 1837, was elected to Congress in 1847, and won the presidential election of 1860 after several failed attempts at gaining a Senate bid.

The Civil War broke out shortly after Lincoln took office. Among the many highlights of his term in office were the Gettysburg Address and the Emancipation Proclamation (both contained in this book). Lincoln was reelected in 1864, but his second term was cut short when he died as a result of assassin John Wilkes Booth's bullet on April 9, 1865. It was only 5 days after General Robert E. Lee had surrendered to Union forces, thus ending the Civil War.

ANDREW JOHNSON (1865-1869)

As a mayor (1830), state representative and senator (1835-1843), congressman (1843-1853), governor of Tennessee (1853-1857), U.S. senator (1857-1862), vice president (1861-1865), and finally president, Andrew Johnson certainly had a long and varied political career. Succeeding Lincoln, Johnson had a rough time of it, barely surviving an impeachment by the House. Born on December 29, 1808, he died on July 31, 1875.

ULYSSES SIMPSON GRANT (1869-1877)

Born on April 27, 1822, this Westpoint graduate fought in the Mexican War and was a brigadier general during the Civil War. Lincoln named him commander-in-chief of the Union forces after his victory at Chattanooga, and he accepted the surrender of Robert E. Lee.

Elected as president in 1868 and reelected in 1872, he lost all of his money when the Grant & Ward investment house collapsed in 1884. His personal memoirs, written while he was dying of cancer, were completed only 4 days before his death. They went on to earn nearly $500,000 in sales.

RUTHERFORD BIRCHARD HAYES (1877-1881)

The 19th president was born on October 4, 1822. A much-awarded major general during the

Civil War, he served in Congress (1864-1867), the governor of Ohio from 1867-1871 and 1875-1877, and after a controversial vote count, was elected president in 1876. He quickly acted to end the Reconstruction era in the South, and died on January 17, 1893.

JAMES ABRAM GARFIELD (1881-1885)

A former farmer, carpenter, and canal bargeman, James Garfield was born on November 19, 1831. Serving as both a state senator (1859) and Congressman (1863), he was the senator-elect in 1880 when he gained the executive office. His term was cut short when a mentally disturbed office-seeker, Charles J. Guiteau, gunned him down on September 19, 1881 in a Washington railroad station.

CHESTER ALAN ARTHUR (1881-1885)

This native of Vermont was born on October 5, 1829. Given the vice presidency in an attempt to placate powerful enemies of Garfield, he found himself with the highest office in the land when the president was assassinated. He died on November 18, 1886.

GROVER CLEVELAND (1885-1889) (1893-1897)

An assistant district attorney (1863), sheriff (1871), mayor, (1881), and governor of New York (1882),

Grover Cleveland was born on March 18, 1837. Famous for battling corruption, Cleveland was elected to the presidency in 1884. While his popular vote was larger, he was defeated in his reelection bid by Benjamin Harrison. However, he won the next election, in 1892, and survived difficult economic times during his four year term. He died on June 24, 1908.

BENJAMIN HARRISON (1889-1893)

Born on August 20, 1833 into a family with a grand political heritage—Harrison's great-grandfather signed the Declaration of Independence, his grandfather was the 9th president of the U.S., and his father was a Congressman—Benjamin Harrison was a civilian lawyer and then a brevet brigadier general during the Civil War. After successful terms as both governor of Indiana (1876) and senator (1881), he won the presidential election in 1888. Six states were admitted during his tenure. He died on March 13, 1901.

WILLIAM McKINLEY (1897-1901)

The 25th president of the U.S., William McKinley was born on January 29, 1843. After a successful stint in the army during the Civil War, McKinley served in the House of Representatives from 1877-1883 and 1885-1891. During that period, he was also the governor of Ohio (1892-1896). He beat William Jennings Bryan in the presidential race of 1896. During his time in office, he demanded Spain's withdrawal from Cuba, which led to the Spanish-American War. Reelected in 1900, his second term ended abruptly when anarchist Leon Czolgosz assassinated him in Buffalo, N.Y. He died on September 14, 1901.

THEODORE ROOSEVELT (1901-1909)

A graduate of Harvard, Theodore Roosevelt was born on October 27, 1858. Roosevelt held a variety of lower-level political positions before organizing the 1st U.S. Volunteer Cavalry, or Rough Riders, as the assistant secretary of the Navy. He led the charge up Kettle Hill in San Juan, Cuba during the Spanish-American War. Returning home a hero, Roosevelt was elected governor of New York (1898-1900).

As vice president under McKinley, Roosevelt took over the office of president upon McKinley's assassination. Under his leadership, anti-trust laws were upheld, the Pure Food and Drugs Act (1906) was enacted, and he paved the way for the Panama Canal. A Nobel Peace Prize winner in 1905 for his mediation between Japan and Russia, he was reelected in 1904. Roosevelt died on January 6, 1919.

WILLIAM HOWARD TAFT (1909-1913)

Groomed his whole life for a high political office,

William Howard Taft graduated from Cincinnati Law School in 1880. A variety of legislative jobs ensued, including assistant prosecuting attorney (1881-1883), superior court judge (1887), and federal circuit judge (1892). After stints as secretary of war (1904) and provisional governor of Cuba (1906), Taft was elected president in 1908.

During his term he dissolved Standard Oil and the tobacco trusts, and instituted the Department of Labor. His fine political career ended with a long run as the chief justice of the U.S. Supreme Court (1921-1930). Born on September 15, 1857, Taft died on March 8, 1930.

WOODROW WILSON (1913-1921)

After a long career in academics—he was the president of Princeton from 1902-1910—Woodrow Wilson became governor of New Jersey in 1911. In 1912, he won the presidential election when the Republican vote was split between Taft and Roosevelt. By keeping America out of war with his hard-line stance, he was reelected in 1916. However, the U.S. entered World War I in 1917.

In 1918, Wilson drafted his "Fourteen Points," a doctrine of self-determination which to this day continues to define how countries around the world view territorial disputes. It also helped end World War I. He helped negotiate the Treaty of Versailles, which contained provisions for the formation of the League of Nations, the forerunner to the United Nations.

Despite suffering a stroke in 1919, Wilson remained in power, and he was awarded the Nobel Peace Prize that same year. Born on December 28, 1856, Wilson died on February 3, 1924.

WARREN GAMALIEL HARDING (1921-1923)

Born on November 2, 1865, Warren Harding went on to become a state senator (1900-1904), lieutenant governor (1904-1906), and U.S. senator (1915). He was elected president in 1920, but his administration was rocked by the Teapot Dome scandal. He died on August 2, 1923.

CALVIN COOLIDGE (1923-1929)

Our 30th president was born on July 4, 1872. He quickly rose through the ranks of politics, going from mayor to state senator to lieutenant governor to governor of Massachusetts. He was well-known for bringing in the state guard during a Boston police strike, and was elected president in 1924. Perhaps his greatest presidential accomplishment was in reducing the national debt by $2 billion over 3 years. He refused to run for a second term and died on January 5, 1933.

HERBERT CLARK HOOVER (1929-1933)

This Stanford graduate was born on August 10, 1874. Hoover was able to travel throughout the world, first as a mining engineer, then as a director of food relief programs for a variety of countries. After a long stint as secretary of commerce, Hoover was elected president in 1928. The stock market crash and subsequent depression marred his years in office. He was defeated in 1932 by Franklin Roosevelt. He died on October 20, 1964.

FRANKLIN DELANO ROOSEVELT (1933-1945)

One of the most popular presidents in the history of the U.S.—his legendary "fireside chats" were a great source of comfort to the nation—Franklin Roosevelt was born on January 30, 1882. After graduating from Columbia Law School, he entered the N.Y. Senate. In 1913 he was appointed as the assistant secretary of the navy. A run for vice president failed in 1920, and in 1921 Roosevelt contracted polio, which left his legs paralyzed.

The future 32nd president was elected as governor of New York in 1928 and 1930. He won the 1932 presidential election, partially on the strength of his promise to repeal prohibition. Roosevelt fought the depression with his New Deal plan, and was subsequently elected to a second, third, and fourth term, the latter despite his failing health. He took part in many strategy meetings with the allied heads of state during World War II, and died on April 12, 1945.

HARRY S. TRUMAN (1945-1953)

The man who authorized the first uses of the atomic bomb was born on May 8, 1884. He held a variety of jobs in his younger years, including newspaper reporter, railroad timekeeper, and farmer, before taking part as a lieutenant in World War I.

Truman was elected U.S. senator in 1934 and 1940, and became vice president in 1944. He took over for Roosevelt when the latter died in office, and soon after made the decision to drop the bombs on Hiroshima and Nagasaki, effectively ending World War II. He created NATO, the Marshall Plan, and the Truman Doctrine, broke the Russian blockade of West Berlin with the famous airlift, and sent General MacArthur after North Korea. Truman died on December 26, 1972.

DWIGHT DAVID EISENHOWER (1953-1961)

A graduate of West Point, this future general of the army and commander of NATO forces was born on October 14, 1890. Eisenhower's long and successful military career formed the basis for his enormously popular war memoirs, *Crusade In Europe,* which helped him gain the voter's nod in the 1952 and 1956 presidential elections. After two busy terms in office, Eisenhower retired, but he continued to act as an advisor to the three presidents who succeeded him. He died on March 28, 1969.

JOHN FITZGERALD KENNEDY (1961-1963)

Born on May 29, 1917, John F. Kennedy went on to become a highly awarded Navy and Marine Corps officer. His book, *Profiles In Courage,* was a Pulitzer prize-winner. Kennedy served in Congress from 1947-1953, was elected to the Senate in 1952 and 1958, and defeated Richard Nixon in the 1960 presidential election.

1961 proved to be a rough year for Kennedy and his administration, as an attempted invasion of Cuba failed. In 1962, Kennedy' hard-line stance against the Russian presence in Cuba was successful, as he forced the USSR to dismantle its missile bases on the nearby island. A supporter of civil rights, medical care, mental health programs, and space flights, Kennedy was assassinated in Dallas on November 22, 1963.

LYNDON BAINES JOHNSON (1963-1969)

The nation's 36th president was born on August 27, 1908. A four term representative, Johnson was elected U.S. senator in 1948 and 1954. He became the president when Kennedy was assassinated, and fought for civil rights, tax reductions, and welfare legislation. However, his political career was marred by his handling of the Vietnam War, and he did not seek reelection in 1968. He died on January 22, 1973.

RICHARD MILLHOUS NIXON (1969-1974)

The only president to resign before completing his term in office, Richard Nixon was born on January 9, 1913. He was elected to the House of Representatives in 1946 and 1948, and to the Senate in 1950. An up and down political career saw Nixon win the vice presidency in 1952 and 1956, but lose 1960 presidential election and the 1962 California race for governor. In 1968, Nixon was elected president.

Highlights of Nixon's presidency included his visits to China and Russia, and his cease-fire agreement with and withdrawal of troops from Vietnam. He also appointed 4 Supreme Court justices, including the chief justice. Nixon's second term was rocked by scandals, most notably the Watergate break-in, which eventually resulted on his resignation on August 9, 1974.

GERALD RUDOLPH FORD (1974-1977)

Born July 14, 1913, Gerald Ford graduated from Yale Law School in 1941. He served as a lieutenant commanded in the navy during World War II, and entered Congress in 1949, where he proceeded to serve for 25 years, 8 of them as the

Republican leader.

Nixon nominated Ford for the vice presidency upon Spiro T. Agnew's resignation in 1973, and became president when Nixon resigned on August 9, 1974. Ford pardoned Nixon almost immediately upon entering office, and was defeated by Jimmy Carter in the 1976 election.

JAMES EARL CARTER (1977-1981)

The former peanut farmer from Georgia was born on October 1, 1924. After a stint in the state senate, Jimmy Carter was elected in 1970 as the governor of Georgia, and went on to defeat Gerald Ford in the 1976 presidential election. The highlight of his term in office was the role he played in the peace negotiations between Israel and Egypt. His administration was plagued by the hostage crisis in Iran. Carter was defeated by Ronald Reagan in the 1980 presidential election.

RONALD WILSON REAGAN (1981-1989)

Our 40th president was born on February 6, 1911. After working as a sports announcer, Reagan became a popular film and television actor. He gradually became active in politics, eventually becoming governor of California in 1966; he was reelected in 1970.

In 1980, Reagan won the presidential election with a landslide victory over Jimmy Carter. He was reelected in 1984 at the age of 73, the oldest man ever elected to the executive office. Highlights of Reagan's presidency included his budget and tax legislation, the summit meetings with Soviet leader Mikhail Gorbachev, and the general economic prosperity the nation experienced under his leadership. Lowlights included high budget deficits and the Iran-Contra affair. Reagan survived an assassination attempt in 1981, as well as major surgeries in 1985 and 1987.

GEORGE HERBERT WALKER BUSH (1989-)

The nation's current president was born on June 12, 1924. A distinguished pilot during World War II, Bush went on to find a successful oil company in Texas. He was elected to the House of Representatives in 1966 and 1968, served as the U.S. ambassador to the United Nations in 1971-1973, and was the director of the CIA from 1976-1977. After serving as Reagan's vice president, he defeated Michael Dukakis in the 1988 presidential election.

VICE PRESIDENTS OF THE UNITED STATES

Name	President Served	Birth & Death
1) John Adams	George Washington	1735-1826
2) Thomas Jefferson	John Adams	1743-1826
3) Aaron Burr	Thomas Jefferson	1756-1836
4) George Clinton	Thomas Jefferson James Madison	1739-1812
5) Elbridge Gerry	James Madison	1744-1814
6) Daniel D. Tompkins	James Madison	1774-1825
7) John C. Calhoun	John Quincy Adams Andrew Jackson	1782-1850
8) Martin Van Buren	Andrew Jackson	1782-1862
9) Richard M. Johnson	Martin Van Buren	1780-1850
10) John Tyler	William H. Harrison	1790-1862
11) George M. Dallas	James K. Polk	1792-1864
12) Millard Fillmore	Zachary Taylor	1800-1874
13) William R. King	Franklin Pierce	1786-1853

Name	President Served	Birth & Death
14) John C. Breckinridge	James Buchanan	1821-1875
15) Hannibal Hamlin	Abraham Lincoln	1809-1891
16) Andrew Johnson	Abraham Lincoln	1808-1875
17) Schuyler Colfax	Ulysses S. Grant	1823-1885
18) Henry Wilson	Ulysses S. Grant	1812-1875
19) William A. Wheeler	Rutherford B. Hayes	1819-1887
20) Chester A. Arthur	James Garfield	1829-1886
21) Thomas A. Hendricks	Grover Cleveland	1819-1885
22) Levi P. Morton	Benjamin Harrison	1824-1920
23) Adlai E. Stevenson	Grover Cleveland	1835-1914
24) Garret A. Hobart	William McKinley	1844-1899
25) Theodore Roosevelt	William McKinley	1858-1919
26) Charles W. Fairbanks	Theodore Roosevelt	1852-1918
27) James S. Sherman	William H. Taft	1855-1912

Name	President Served	Birth & Death
28) Thomas R. Marshall	Woodrow Wilson	1854-1925
29) Calvin Coolidge	Warren G. Harding	1872-1933
30) Charles G. Dawes	Calvin Coolidge	1865-1951
31) Charles Curtis	Herbert C. Hoover	1860-1936
32) John N. Garner	Franklin D. Roosevelt	1868-1967
33) Henry A. Wallace	Franklin D. Roosevelt	1888-1965
34) Harry S. Truman	Franklin D. Roosevelt	1884-1972
35) Alben W. Barkley	Harry S. Truman	1877-1956
36) Richard M. Nixon	Dwight D. Eisenhower	1913-
37) Lyndon B. Johnson	John F. Kennedy	1908-1973
38) Hubert H. Humphrey	Lyndon B. Johnson	1911-1978
39) Spiro T. Agnew	Richard M. Nixon	1918-
40) Gerald R. Ford	Richard M. Nixon	1913-
41) Nelson A. Rockefeller	Gerald R. Ford	1908-1979

Name	President Served	Birth & Death
42) Walter F. Mondale	Jimmy Carter	1928-
43) George Bush	Ronald Reagan	1924-
44) J. Danforth Quayle	George Bush	1947-

FACTS ABOUT THE 50 STATES

State: Alabama
Capital: Montgomery
Settled: 1702
Date Entered Union: December 14, 1819
Number: 22
Origin/Meaning Of Name: Originally the Indian name for "tribal town," this area was later the home to a tribe (Alabamas or Alibamons) of the Creek confederacy.
Nickname: Heart of Dixie; Camellia State
Flower: Camellia
Bird: Yellowhammer
Motto: "We dare defend our rights"
Postal Abbreviation: AL

State: Alaska
Capital: Juneau
Settled: January 3, 1959
Date Entered Union: 1784
Number: 49
Origin/Meaning Of Name: Russian translation of the Aleutian (Eskimo) word, "alakshak," meaning "great lands," "peninsula," or "land that is not an island."
Nickname: The Last Frontier
Flower: Forget-me-not
Bird: Willow ptarmigan
Motto: "North to the future"
Postal Abbreviation: AK

State: Arizona
Capital: Phoenix
Settled: February 14, 1912
Date Entered Union: 1776
Number: 48
Origin/Meaning Of Name: Either from the Spanish version of the Pima Indian word for "little spring place," or their translation of the Aztec word "arizuma," which means "sliver-bearing."
Nickname: Grand Canyon State
Flower: Saguaro
Bird: Cactus wren
Motto: "Diat Deus" ("God enriches")
Postal Abbreviation: AZ

State: Arkansas
Capital: Little Rock
Settled: 1686
Date Entered Union: June 15, 1836
Number: 25
Origin/Meaning Of Name: French derivative of the Siouan Quapaw, Indians whose name means "downstream people."
Nickname: Land Of Opportunity
Flower: Apple blossom
Bird: Mockingbird
Motto: "Regnat populus" ("The people rule")
Postal Abbreviation: AR

State: California
Capital: Sacramento
Settled: 1769
Date Entered Union: September 9, 1850
Number: 31
Origin/Meaning Of Name: Bestowed by the Spanish conquistadors (possibly Cortez). It was the name of a fictitious earthly paradise, in *Las Serges de Esplandian,* a Spanish romance written by Montalvo in 1510.
Nickname: Golden State
Flower: Golden poppy
Bird: California valley quail
Motto: "Eureka" ("I have found it")
Postal Abbreviation: CA

State: Colorado
Capital: Denver
Settled: 1858
Date Entered Union: August 1, 1876
Number: 38
Origin/Meaning Of Name: A Spanish word for "red," originally applied to the Colorado River.
Nickname: Centennial State
Flower: Blue columbine
Bird: Lark bunting
Motto: "Nil sie numine" ("Nothing without providence")
Postal Abbreviation: CO

State: Connecticut
Capital: Hartford
Settled: 1634
Dated Entered Union: January 9, 1788
Number: 5
Origin/Meaning Of Name: From the Mohican and Algonquin Indian word meaning "long river place."
Nickname: Constitution State; Nutmeg State
Flower: Mountain laurel
Bird: American robin
Motto: "Qui transtulit sustinet" ("He who transplanted still sustains")
Postal Abbreviation: CT

State: Delaware
Capital: Dover
Settled: 1638
Date Entered Union: December 7, 1787
Number: 1
Origin/Meaning Of Name: A version of the name of Lord De La Warr, an early governor of Virginia, it was first applied to the Delaware River, then to a local Indian tribe (Lenni-Lenape), and finally to the state itself.
Nickname: First State; Diamond State
Flower: Peach blossom
Bird: Blue hen chicken
Motto: "Liberty and independence"
Postal Abbreviation: DE

State: Florida
Capital: Tallahassee
Settled: 1565
Date Entered Union: March 3, 1845
Number: 27
Origin/Meaning Of Name: Named by Ponce de Leon on Easter Sunday, 1513, it means "flowery easter," or "feast of flowers."
Nickname: Sunshine State
Flower: Orange blossom
Bird: Mockingbird
Motto: "In God we trust"
Postal Abbreviation: FL

State: Georgia
Capital: Atlanta
Settled: 1733
Date Entered Union: January 2, 1788
Number: 4
Origin/Meaning Of Name: Named for King George II of England by James Oglethorpe, who was granted a charter by the King to found the colony of Georgia in 1732.
Nickname: Empire State Of The South; Peace State
Flower: Cherokee rose
Bird: Brown thrasher
Motto: "Wisdom, justice, and moderation"
Postal Abbreviation: GA

State: Hawaii
Capital: Honolulu
Settled: 1820
Date Entered Union: August 21, 1959
Number: 50
Origin/Meaning Of Name: Possibly derived from the native word "hawaiki" or "owhyhee," meaning "homeland."
Nickname: Aloha State
Flower: Hibiscus
Bird: Nene goose
Motto: "The life of the land is perpetuated in righteousness"
Postal Abbreviation: HI

State: Idaho
Capital: Boise
Settled: 1842
Date Entered Union: July 3, 1890
Number: 43
Origin/Meaning Of Name: A coined name with an invented Indian meaning: "gem of the mountains," or "light on the mountains." Some historians feel that the name may be a Kiowa Apache term for the Comanche.
Nickname: Gem State
Flower: Syringa
Bird: Mountain bluebird
Motto: "Esto perpetua" ("It is perpetual")
Postal Abbreviation: ID

State: Illinois
Capital: Springfield
Settled: 1720
Date Entered Union: December 3, 1818
Number: 21
Origin/Meaning Of Name: French for "Illini," an Algonquin word meaning "men" or "soldiers."
Nickname: Prairie State
Flower: Native violet
Bird: Cardinal
Motto: "State sovereignty—national union"
Postal Abbreviation: IL

State: Indiana
Capital: Indianapolis
Settled: 1733
Date Entered Union: December 11, 1816
Number: 19
Origin/Meaning Of Name: Settlers named the territory. It means "land of the Indians."
Nickname: Hoosier State
Flower: Peony
Bird: Cardinal
Motto: "Crossroads of America"
Postal Abbreviation: IN

State: Iowa
Capital: Des Moines
Settled: 1788
Date Entered Union: December 28, 1846
Number: 29
Origin/Meaning Of Name: A Sioux word that has been variously translated as "one who puts to sleep" or "beautiful land."
Nickname: Hawkeye State
Flower: Wild rose
Bird: Goldfinch
Motto: "Our liberties we prize and our rights we will maintain"
Postal Abbreviation: IA

State: Kansas
Capital: Topeka
Settled: 1727
Date Entered Union: January 29, 1861
Number: 34
Origin/Meaning Of Name: From the Sioux word for those people who lived in the south, i.e., "south wind people."
Nickname: Sunflower State
Flower: Sunflower
Bird: Western meadowlark
Motto: "Ad astra per asepera" ("To the stars through difficulties")
Postal Abbreviation: KS

State: Kentucky
Capital: Frankfort
Settled: 1774
Date Entered Union: June 1, 1792
Number: 15
Origin/Meaning Of Name: Indian word that has been variously translated as meaning "dark and bloody ground," "meadow land," or "land of tomorrow."
Nickname: Bluegrass State
Flower: Goldenrod
Bird: Kentucky cardinal
Motto: "United we stand, divided we fall"
Postal Abbreviation: KY

State: Louisiana
Capital: Baton Rouge
Settled: 1699
Date Entered Union: April 30, 1812
Number: 18
Origin/Meaning Of Name: Part of the original vast territory called Louisiana, named by Sieur de La Salle for the French King Louis XIV.
Nickname: Pelican State
Flower: Magnolia
Bird: Eastern brown pelican
Motto: "Union, justice and confidence"
Postal Abbreviation: LA

State: Maine
Capital: Augusta
Settled: 1624
Date Entered Union: March 15, 1820
Number: 23
Origin/Meaning Of Name: From the French word for "province." It is also a descriptive term, referring to the mainland as distinct from the many coastal islands.
Nickname: Pine Tree State
Flower: Pine cone and tassel
Bird: Chickadee
Motto: "Dirigo" ("I direct")
Postal Abbreviation: ME

State: Maryland
Capital: Annapolis
Settled: 1634
Date Entered Union: April 28, 1788
Number: 7
Origin/Meaning Of Name: Named after Queen Henrietta Maria, the wife of Charles I of England.
Nickname: Old Line State; Free State
Flower: Black-eyed Susan
Bird: Baltimore oriole
Motto: "Fatti maschii, parole femine" ("Manly deeds, womanly words")
Postal Abbreviation: MD

State: Massachusetts
Capital: Boston
Settled: 1620
Date Entered Union: February 6, 1788
Number: 6
Origin/Meaning Of Name: From the name of the Indian tribe that lived near Milton, Mass., it can be translated as "large hill place."
Nickname: Bay State; Colony State
Flower: Mayflower
Bird: Chickadee
Motto: "Ense petit placidam sub liberate" ("By the sword we seek peace, but peace only under liberty)
Postal Abbreviation: MA

State: Michigan
Capital: Lansing
Settled: 1668
Date Entered Union: January 25, 1837
Number: 26
Origin/Meaning Of Name: From the Chippewa word "mici-gama," which means "great water," after the lake of the same name.
Nickname: Great Lake State; Wolverine State
Flower: Apple
Bird: Robin
Motto: "Si quaeris peninsulam amoenam" ("If you seek a pleasant peninsula, look about you")
Postal Abbreviation: MI

State: Minnesota
Capital: St. Paul
Settled: 1805
Date Entered Union: May 11, 1858
Number: 32
Origin/Meaning Of Name: From Dakota Sioux description of the Minnesota River, it means "cloudy water" or "sky-tinted water."
Nickname: North Star State; Gopher State
Flower: Showy lady slipper
Bird: Common loon
Motto: "L'Etoile du nord" ("Star of the north")
Postal Abbreviation: MN

State: Mississippi
Capital: Jackson
Settled: 1699
Date Entered Union: December 10, 1817
Number: 20
Origin/Meaning Of Name: Probably from the Chippewa words "mici" and "zibi," or "great river."
Nickname: Magnolia State
Flower: Magnolia
Bird: Mockingbird
Motto: "Virtute et armis" ("By valor and arms")
Postal Abbreviation: MS

State: Missouri
Capital: Jefferson City
Settled: 1735
Date Entered Union: August 10, 1821
Number: 24
Origin/Meaning Of Name: After the name of an Algonquin Indian tribe who were in turn named after the Missouri River. It means "muddy water."
Nickname: Show-Me State
Flower: Hawthorn
Bird: Bluebird
Motto: "Salus populi suprema lex esto" ("The welfare of the people shall be the supreme law")
Postal Abbreviation: MO

State: Montana
Capital: Helena
Settled: 1809
Date Entered Union: November 8, 1889
Number: 41
Origin/Meaning Of Name: Derived from the Latin or Spanish word for "mountainous."
Nickname: Treasure State
Flower: Bitterroot
Bird: Western meadowlark
Motto: "Oro y plata" ("Gold and silver")
Postal Abbreviation: MT

State: Nebraska
Capital: Lincoln
Settled: 1823
Date Entered Union: March 1, 1867
Number: 37
Origin/Meaning Of Name: From the Omaha or Otos Indian word meaning "broad water" or "flat river," it is descriptive of the Platte River.
Nickname: Cornhusker State
Flower: Goldenrod
Bird: Meadowlark
Motto: "Equality before the law"
Postal Abbreviation: NE

State: Nevada
Capital: Carson City
Settled: 1849
Date Entered Union: October 31, 1864
Number: 36
Origin/Meaning Of Name: The Spanish word for "snow-clad."
Nickname: Sagebrush State; Battle-Born State
Flower: Sagebrush
Bird: Mountain bluebird
Motto: "All for our country"
Postal Abbreviation: NV

State: New Hampshire
Capital: Concord
Settled: 1623
Date Entered Union: June 21, 1788
Number: 9
Origin/Meaning Of Name: Captain John Mason of Plymouth Council named this colony in 1629 after his home county in England.
Nickname: Granite State
Flower: Purple lilac
Bird: Purple finch
Motto: "Live free or die"
Postal Abbreviation: NH

State: New Jersey
Capital: Trenton
Settled: 1664
Date Entered Union: December, 18, 1787
Number: 3
Origin/Meaning Of Name: John Berekely and Sir George Carteret named this territory after England's Isle of Jersey.
Nickname: Garden State
Flower: Purple violet
Bird: Eastern goldfinch
Motto: "Liberty and prosperity"
Postal Abbreviation: NJ

State: New Mexico
Capital: Santa Fe
Settled: 1610
Date Entered Union: January 6, 1912
Number: 47
Origin/Meaning Of Name: Named by the Spanish in the 16th century for the land which lay north and west of the Rio Grande.
Nickname: Land Of Enchantment
Flower: Yucca
Bird: Roadrunner
Motto: "Crescit eundo" ("It grows as it goes")
Postal Abbreviation: NM

State: New York
Capital: Albany
Settled: 1614
Date Entered Union: July 26, 1788
Number: 11
Origin/Meaning Of Name: Originally called New Netherland, it was subsequently named after the Duke of York and Albany, who received a patent to the area from his brother Charles II and sent an expedition to capture it from the Dutch in 1644.
Nickname: Empire State
Flower: Rose
Bird: Bluebird
Motto: "Excelsior" ("Ever Upward")
Postal Abbreviation: NY

State: North Carolina
Capital: Raleigh
Settled: 1660
Date Entered Union: November 21, 1789
Number: 12
Origin/Meaning Of Name: In 1619 Charles I gave a patent to Sir Robert Heath to be called Province of Carolana (from Carolus, the Latin name for Charles).
Nickname: Tar Heel State; Old North State
Flower: Dogwood
Bird: Cardinal
Motto: "Esse quam videri" ("To be rather than to seem")
Postal Abbreviation: NC

State: North Dakota
Capital: Bismarck
Settled: 1812
Date Entered Union: November 2, 1889
Number: 39
Origin/Meaning Of Name: Dakota is the Sioux word for "friend" or "ally."
Nickname: Peace Garden State
Flower: Wild prairie rose
Bird: Western meadowlark
Motto: "Liberty and union, now and forever, one and inseparable"
Postal Abbreviation: ND

State: Ohio
Capital: Columbus
Settled: 1788
Date Entered Union: March 1, 1803
Number: 17
Origin/Meaning Of Name: The Iroquis word for "great, fine, or good river."
Nickname: Buckeye State
Flower: Scarlet carnation
Bird: Cardinal
Motto: "With God, all things are possible"
Postal Abbreviation: OH

State: Oklahoma
Capital: Oklahoma City
Settled: 1889
Date Entered Union: November 16, 1907
Number: 46
Origin/Meaning Of Name: A Choctaw Indian word for "red man," proposed by Rev. Allen Wright, a Choctaw-speaking Indian.
Nickname: Sooner State
Flower: Mistletoe
Bird: Scissor-tailed flycatcher
Motto: "Labor omnia vincit" ("Labor conquers all things")
Postal Abbreviation: OK

State: Oregon
Capital: Salem
Settled: 1811
Date Entered Union: February 14, 1859
Number: 33
Origin/Meaning Of Name: Origin unknown. Some speculate that the name may have been derived from that of the Wisconsin River—called "Ouaricon-sint" on a 1715 Frenchmap. Some feel that the term comes from the Algonquin word "wauregan," which means "beautiful water."
Nickname: Beaver State
Flower: Oregon grape
Bird: Western meadowlark
Motto: "The union"
Postal Abbreviation: OR

State: Pennsylvania
Capital: Harrisburg
Settled: 1682
Date Entered Union: December 12, 1787
Number: 2
Origin/Meaning Of Name: William Penn, the Quaker who was made full proprietor by King Charles II in 1681, suggested the name "Sylvania," or "woodland." However, because the king's government owed Penn's father, Admiral William Penn, 16,000 pounds, the land was granted as partial settlement and Charles II added the Penn to Sylvania, against the desires of the Admiral, in

honor of the man. The literal translation is "Penn's wood."

Nickname: Keystone State
Flower: Mountain laurel
Bird: Ruffed grouse
Motto: "Virtue, liberty and independence"
Postal Abbreviation: PA

State: Rhode Island
Capital: Providence
Settled: 1636
Date Entered Union: May 29, 1790
Number: 13
Origin/Meaning Of Name: Origin unknown. Some believe it was named by Giovanni de Verrazano, who recorded an island about the size of Rhodes in the Mediterranean in 1524. Others theorize that the state was named "Rhode Eylandt" by Dutch Explorer Adriaen Block because of its red clay.
Nickname: Little Rhody; Ocean State
Flower: Violet
Bird: Rhode Island hen
Motto: "Hope"
Postal Abbreviation: RI

State: South Carolina
Capital: Columbia
Settled: 1670
Date Entered Union: May 23, 1788
Number: 8
Origin/Meaning Of Name: See North Carolina
Nickname: Palmetto State
Flower: Carolina jessamine
Bird: Carolina wren
Motto: "Dum spiro spero" ("While I breathe, I hope")
Postal Abbreviation: SC

State: South Dakota
Capital: Pierre
Settled: 1859
Date Entered Union: November 2, 1889
Number: 40
Origin/Meaning Of Name: See North Dakota
Nickname: Coyote State; Sunshine State
Flower: Pasqueflower
Bird: Pheasant
Motto: "Under God, the people rule"
Postal Abbreviation: SD

State: Tennessee
Capital: Nashville
Settled: 1769
Date Entered Union: June 1, 1796
Number: 16
Origin/Meaning Of Name: Named after the Cherokee village of "Tanasi," located on the Little Tennessee River.
Nickname: Volunteer State
Flower: Iris
Bird: Mockingbird
Motto: Agriculture and commerce
Postal Abbreviation: TN

State: Texas
Capital: Austin
Settled: 1682
Date Entered Union: December 28, 1845
Number: 28
Origin/Meaning Of Name: A variant of the Caddo Indian word for "friends" or "allies." It was often also written as "texias," "tejas," "teysas."
Nickname: Lone Star State
Flower: Bluebonnet
Bird: Mockingbird
Motto: "Friendship"
Postal Abbreviation: TX

State: Utah
Capital: Salt Lake City
Settled: 1847
Date Entered Union: January 4, 1896
Number: 45
Origin/Meaning Of Name: From the Navajo word meaning "upper," or "higher up."
Nickname: Beehive State
Flower: Sego Lily
Bird: Seagull
Motto: "Industry"
Postal Abbreviation: UT

State: Vermont
Capital: Montpelier
Settled: 1724
Date Entered Union: March 4, 1791
Number: 14
Origin/Meaning Of Name: The most popular theory holds that Samuel de Champlain named the area using the french words "vert" and "mont," for "green mountain." When the state was formed in 1777, Dr. Thomas Young suggested combining "vert" and "mont" into "Vermont."
Nickname: Green Mountain State
Flower: Red clover
Bird: Thrush
Motto: "Freedom and unity"
Postal Abbreviation: VT

State: Virginia
Capital: Richmond
Settled: 1607
Date Entered Union: June 25, 1788
Number: 10
Origin/Meaning Of Name: Named in 1584 by Sir Walter Raleigh in honor of Queen Elizabeth I, the Virgin Queen of England.
Nickname: Old Dominion
Flower: Flowering dogwood
Bird: Cardinal
Motto: "Sic semper tyrannis" ("Thus always to tyrants")
Postal Abbreviation: VA

State: Washington
Capital: Olympia
Settled: 1811
Date Entered Union: November 11, 1889
Number: 42
Origin/Meaning Of Name: It was originally called the "Territory of Columbia," the name was changed because of the existence of the District of Columbia. Its new name, of course, was chosen in honor of the nation's first president.
Nickname: Evergreen State
Flower: Rhododendron
Bird: Willow goldfinch
Motto: "Alki" ("By and by")
Postal Abbreviation: WA

State: West Virginia
Capital: Charleston
Settled: 1727
Date Entered Union: June 20, 1863
Number: 35
Origin/Meaning Of Name: Named in 1863 when western counties of Virginia refused to secede from the Union.
Nickname: Mountain State
Flower: Big rhododendron
Bird: Cardinal
Motto: "Montani semper liberi" ("Mountaineers are always free")
Postal Abbreviation: WV

State: Wisconsin
Capital: Madison
Settled: 1766
Date Entered Union: May 29, 1848
Number: 30
Origin/Meaning Of Name: A Chippewa word alternately spelled "Ouisconsin" and "Mesconsing" by early explorers, it is believed to mean "grassy place." "Wisconsin" was chosen by Congress when the area became a state.
Nickname: Badger State
Flower: Wood violet
Bird: Robin
Motto: "Forward"
Postal Abbreviation: WI

State: Wyoming
Capital: Cheyenne
Settled: 1834
Date Entered Union: July 10, 1890
Number: 44
Origin/Meaning Of Name: This Alogoniquin word means "large prairie place." The name was taken from Wyoming Valley, Pa., the site of an Indian massacre, and became widely known because of Thomas Campbell's poem, "Gertrude of Wyoming."
Nickname: Equality State
Flower: Indian paintbrush
Bird: Meadowlark
Motto: "Equal rights"
Postal Abbreviation: WY

GEOGRAPHY TRIVIA TEST

Can you name the . . .
(answers follow)

1) largest state?

2) smallest state?

3) largest county (outside of Alaska)?

4) smallest county?

5) Easternmost city?

6) Easternmost point?

7) Westernmost city?

8) Westernmost point?

9) Northernmost city?

10) Northernmost point?

11) Southernmost city?

12) Southernmost point?

13) lowest point?

14) highest waterfall?

15) longest river?

16) deepest lake?

17) rainiest spot?

18) highest mountain?

19) largest gorge?

20) deepest gorge?

21) oldest national park?

22) largest national park?

23) largest national monument?

24) tallest building?

25) largest building?

26) tallest structure?

27) longest bridge span?

28) highest bridge?

29) biggest dam?

ANSWERS:

1) Alaska—591,004 square miles

2) Rhode Island—1,1212 square miles

3) San Bernardino Country, California—20,064 square miles

4) Kalawo, Hawaii—14 square miles

5) Eastport, Maine—66 degrees 59 minutes 02 seconds West

6) Quoddy Head, Maine—66 degrees 57 minutes West

7) Unalaska, Alaska—166 degrees 32 minutes West

8) Cape Wrangell, Alaska—172 degrees 27 minutes East

9) Barrow, Alaska—71 degrees 17 minutes North

10) Point Barrow, Alaska—71 degrees 23 minutes North

11) Hilo, Hawaii—19 degrees 43 minutes North

12) Ka Lae (South Cape), Island of Hawaii—18 degrees 55 minutes North

13) Death Valley, California—282 feet

14) Yosemite Falls—2,425 feet

15) Mississippi-Missouri—3,710 miles

16) Crater Lake, Oregon—1,932 feet

17) Mt. Waialeale, Hawaii—460 inches of rain per year

18) Mount McKinley, Alaska—20,320 feet

19) Grand Canyon, Colorado River, Arizona—277 miles long, 600 feet to 18 miles wide, 1 mile deep

20) Hell's Canyon, Snake River, Idaho-Oregon—7,900 feet

21) Yellowstone National Park—1872

22) Wrangell-St. Elias, Alaska—13,018 square miles

23) Death Valley—3,231 square miles

24) Sears Tower, Chicago, Illinois—1,454 feet

25) Boeing 747 Manufacturing Plant, Everett, Washington—205,600,000 cubic feet or 47 acres

26) TV tower, Blanchard, North Dakota—2,063 feet

27) Verrazano-Narrows, New York—4,260 feet

28) Royal Gorge, Colorado—1,053 feet above water

29) New Cornelia Tailings, Ten Mile Wash, Arizona—274,026,000 cubic yards of material used

THE DECLARATION OF INDEPENDENCE

Written almost solely by Thomas Jefferson, the Declaration of Independence announced the separation of the thirteen colonies from Britain, as well as their creation of the United States of America. One of the greatest political documents in history, it clearly states the American ideal of government, based on an abstract theory of human rights.

The Declaration of Independence

THE DECLARATION OF INDEPENDENCE

In Congress, July 4, 1776

The Unanimous Declaration of the Thirteen United States of America

When in the Course of human events, it becomes necessary for one people to dissolve the political bands which have connected them with another, and to assume among the powers of the earth, the separate and equal station to which the Laws of Nature and of Nature's God entitle them, a decent respect to the opinions of mankind requires that they should declare the causes which impel them to the separation.

We hold these truths to be self-evident, that all men are created equal, that they are endowed by their Creator with certain unalienable Rights, that among these are Life, Liberty and the pursuit of Happiness. That to secure these rights, Governments are instituted among Men, deriving their just powers from the consent of the governed. That whenever any Form of Government becomes destructive of these ends it is the Right of the People to alter or to abolish it, and to institute new Government, laying its foundation on such principles and organizing its powers in such form, as to them shall seem most likely to effect their Safety and Happiness. Prudence, indeed, will dictate that Governments long established should not be changed for light and transient causes; and accordingly all experience hath shewn, that mankind are more disposed to suffer, while evils are sufferable, than to right themselves by abolishing the forms to which they are accustomed. But when a long train of abuses and usurpations, pursuing invariably the same Object evinces a design to reduce them under absolute Despotism, it is their right, it is their duty, to throw off such Government, and to provide new Guards for their future security. Such has been the patient sufferance of these Colonies; and such is now the necessity which constrains them to alter their former Systems of Government. The history of the present King of Great Britain is a history of repeated injuries and usurpations, all having in direct object the establishment of an absolute Tyranny over these States. To prove this, let Facts be submitted to a candid world.

He has refused his Assent to Laws, the most wholesome and necessary for the public good.

He has forbidden his Governors to pass Laws of

immediate and pressing importance, unless suspended in their operation till his Assent should be obtained; and when so suspended, he has utterly neglected to attend to them.

He has refused to pass other Laws for the accommodation of large districts of people, unless those people would relinquish the right of Representation in the legislature, a right inestimable to them and formidable to tyrants only.

He has called together legislative bodies at places unusual, uncomfortable, and distant from the depository of their public Records, for the sole purpose of fatiguing them into compliance with his measures.

He has dissolved Representative Houses repeatedly, for opposing with manly firmness his invasions on the rights of the people.

He has refused for a long time, after such dissolutions, to cause others to be elected; whereby the Legislative powers, incapable of Annihilation, have returned to the People at large for their exercise; the State remaining in the mean time exposed to all the dangers of invasion from without, and convulsions within.

He has endeavoured to prevent the population of these states; for the purpose obstructing the Laws for Naturalization of Foreigners; refusing to pass others to encourage their migrations hither, and raising the conditions of new Appropriations of Lands.

He has obstructed the Administration of Justice, by refusing his Assent to Laws for establishing Judiciary powers.

He has made Judges dependent on his Will alone, for the tenure of their offices, and the amount and payment of their salaries.

He has erected a multitude of New Offices, and sent hither swarms of Officers to harrass our people, and eat out their substance.

He has kept among us, in times of peace, standing Armies without the consent of our legislatures.

He has affected to render the military independent of and superior to the Civil power.

He has combined with others to subject us to a jurisdiction foreign to our constitution, and unacknowledged by our laws; giving his Assent to their Acts of pretended Legislation:

For Quartering large bodies of armed troops among us:

For protecting them, by a mock Trial, from punishment for any Murders which they should commit on the Inhabitants of these States:

For cutting off our Trade with all parts of the world:

For imposing Taxes on us without our Consent:

For depriving us in many cases of the benefits of Trial by Jury:

For transporting us beyond Seas to be tried for pretended offences:

For abolishing the free System of English Laws in a neighbouring Province, establishing therein an Arbitrary government, and enlarging its Boundaries so as to render it at once an example and fit instrument for introducing the same absolute rule into these Colonies:

For taking away our Charters, abolishing our most valuable Laws, and altering fundamentally the Forms of our Governments:

For suspending our own Legislatures, and declarin themselves invested with power to legislate for us in all cases whatsoever.

He has abdicated Government here, by declaring us out of his Protection and waging war against us.

He has plundered our seas, ravaged our Coasts, burnt our towns, and destroyed the Lives of our people.

He is at this time transporting large Armies of foreign Mercenaries to complete the works of death, desolation and tyranny, already begun with circumstances of Cruelty & Perfidy scarcely paralleled in the most barbarous ages, and totally unworthy the Head of a civilized nation.

He has constrained our fellow Citizens taken Captive on the high Seas to bear Arms against their Country, to become the executioners of their friends and Brethren, or to fall themselves by their Hands.

He has excited domestic insurrections amongst us, and has endeavoured to bring on the inhabitants of our frontiers, the merciless Indian Savages, whose known rule or warfare, is an undistinguished destruction of all ages, sexes and conditions.

In every stage of these Oppressions We have Petitioed for Redress in the most humble terms: Our repeated Petitions have been answered only by repeated injury. A Prince, whose character is thus marked by every act which may define a Tyrant, is unfit to be the ruler of a free people.

Nor have We been wanting in attentions to our British brethren. We have warned them from time to time of attempts by their legislature to extend an unwarrantable jurisdiction over us. We have reminded them of the circumstances of our emigration and settlement here. We have appealed to their native justice and magnanimity, and we have conjured them by the ties of our common kindred to disavow these usurpations, which, would inevitably interrupt our connections and corespondence. They too have been deaf to the voice of justice and of consanguinity. We must, therefore, acquiesce in the necessity, which denounces our Separation, and hold them, as we hold the rest of mankind, Enemies in War, in Peace Friends.

We, therefore, the Representatives of the UNITED STATES OF AMERICA, in General Congress, Assembled, appealing to the Supreme Judge of the world for the rectitude of our intentions, do, in the Name, and by Authority of the good People of these Colonies, solemnly publish and declare, That these United Colonies are, and of Right ought to be Free and Independent States; that they are Absolved from all Allegiance to the British Crown, and that all political connection between them and the State of Great Britain, is and ought to be totally dissolved; and that as Free and Independent States, they have full Power to levy War, conclude Peace, contract Alliances, establish Commerce, and to do all other Acts and Things which Independent States may of right do. And for the support of this Declaration, with a firm reliance on the protection of divine Providence, we mutually pledge to each other our Lives, our Fortunes and our sacred Honor.

John Hancock, President, Continental Congress

Button Gwinnett	Thos. Nelson Jr.	Richd. Stockton
Lyman Hall	Francis Lightfoot Lee	Jno Witherspoon
Geo Walton.	Carter Braxton	Fras. Hopkinson
Wm. Hooper	Robt. Morris	John Hart
Joseph Hewes	Benjamin Rush	Abra Clark
John Penn	Benja. Franklin	Josiah Bartlett
Edward Rutledge	John Morton	Wm. Whipple
Thos. Heyward Junr.	Geo Clymer	Saml. Adams

Thomas Lynch Junr. Jas. Smith. John Adams
Arthur Middleton Geo. Taylor Robt. Treat Paine
Samuel Chase James Wilson Elbridge Gerry
Wm. Paca Geo. Ross Step. Hopkins
Thos. Stone Caesar Rodney William Ellery
Charles Carroll Tho. McKean Saml Huntington
  of Carrollton
George Wythe Wm. Floyd Wm. Williams
Richard Henry Lee Phil. Livingston Oliver Wolcott
Th. Jefferson Frans. Lewis Matthew Thorton
Benja. Harrison Lewis Morris

THE CONSTITUTION OF THE UNITED STATES

This famous document, which establishes a federal republic with sovereignty balanced between the national government and the individual states, embodies the principles on which the United States of America is governed. It is the supreme law of the land, and no other law can operate if it conflicts with what is written in the constitution. The document was composed at the Federal Constitutional Convention of 1787, and ratified by nine states on June 21, 1788. The Preamble effectively states the general purpose of the Constitution.

Preamble to the Constitution of the United States of America

WE THE PEOPLE of the United States, in order to form a more perfect Union, establish justice, insure domestic tranquility, provide for the common defense, promote the general welfare, and secure the blessings of liberty to ourselves and our posterity, do ordain and establish this Constitution for the United States of America.

Summary of the 7 Articles and 26 Amendments

Article I

This article places all legislative powers in a bicameral Congress that is made up by a Senate and House of Representatives. It also prescribes a method of electing a Congress, and provides each house with the power to establish its own procedural rules. The process of legislation from the Congress to the President is described. Section VIII grants Congress specific powers, for instance, the power to declare war. Section IX limits Congressional powers, forbidding, for instance, ex post facto laws. Section X limits the powers of states, and makes certain state actions dependent on Congressional consent.

Article II

Article two creates the Executive branch of the government, to be headed by a President and Vice President. It also establishes the Electoral College, outlines the election process, qualifications, and manner of succession when a President is incapacitated. Section II lists the President's powers as military commander-in-chief and as related to foreign affairs. Section III addresses the President's working relations with Congress and grants the President administrative power. Section IV governs the impeachment of a President.

Article III

The third article vests all judicial power in a Supreme Court. It also states that Congress can establish inferior courts. Section II defines the extent of federal jurisdiction, and distinguishes cases in which federal jurisdiction is original—for instance, cases between states—from those in which the federal courts can only hear appeals. Section III defines and limits prosecution for treason.

Article IV

This article addresses relations between states, such as prescribing full faith and credit for one another's laws, equal treatment for the citizens of all states, and extradition procedures. Section III governs the admission of states to the Union, as well as the administration of federal land. Section IV guarantees every state a republican form of government.

Article V

Article five outlines the process of amending the Constitution.

Article VI

The sixth article establishes the Constitution as the supreme law of the land, regardless of any conflicting state laws. It also asserts that Federal and state officeholders shall be bound to support the Constitution, and that no religious test may be demanded as a qualification for office.

Article VII

Article seven simply says that the Constitution will take effect when nine of the thirteen states ratify it.

Amendment I

The first Bill of Rights amendment prohibits government-established religion, and guarantees the freedom of worship, speech, the press, assembly, and the right to petition the government. (1791)

Amendment II

This amendment was passed in order to guarantee the maintenance of a well-regulated militia, as well as to preserve the right to keep and bear arms. (1791)

Amendment III

The third amendment prohibits the peacetime quartering of troops in private dwellings without their owners' consent. (1791)

Amendment IV

Number four provides guarantees against unreasonable search and seizure. (1791)

Amendment V

This amendment provides guarantees against violations of due process in criminal proceedings. It states that no person can be compelled to testify against himself. Additionally, the amendment asserts that a grand jury process is required for criminal indictment. It prohibits double jeopardy, and says that the public taking of private property without just compensation is prohibited. (1791)

Amendment VI

The sixth amendment guarantees a speedy and fair trial, an impartial jury, and the right to counsel in all criminal cases. (1791)

Amendment VII

Number seven guarantees a jury trial in all major civil, or noncriminal, cases. It also prohibits the retrial of adjudicated matters. (1791)

Amendment VIII

This amendment prohibits excessive bail or fines, as well as cruel and unusual punishment. (1791)

Amendment IX

Amendment nine states that the enumeration of certain rights in the Constitution does not mean that the people do not retain all other rights. (1791)

Amendment X

This amendment gives the states powers that the Constitution does not give to the federal government or prohibit to the states. (1791)

Amendment XI

Number 11 states that federal courts can not try any case brought against a state by a citizen of another state or country. (1798)

Amendment XII

The twelfth amendment revises the rules for presidential and vice presidential elections. (1804)

Amendment XIII

Number 13 was the first of three "Civil War" amendments. It prohibits slavery. (1865)

Amendment XIV

This amendment provides a definition of U.S. citizenship. It also prohibits states from violating due process or equal protection of the law. (1868)

Amendment XV

The fifteenth amendment guarantees the rights of citizens against U.S. or state infringement based on race, color, or previous servitude. (1870)

Amendment XVI

Number 16 provides authorization for a federal income tax. (1913)

Amendment XVII

Amendment 17 provides for the direct popular election of Senators. (1913)

Amendment XVIII

This amendment makes Prohibition a federal law. (1919)

Amendment XIX

The nineteenth amendment guarantees women the right to vote in state and U.S. elections. (1920)

Amendment XX

Number 20 provides for changes in the Congressional terms of office and the inauguration date of President and Vice President. It also clarifies the rules of succession to the presidency. (1933)

Amendment XXI

The twenty-first amendment repeals Amendment XVIII, thus ending Prohibition. (1933)

Amendment XXII

Number 22 limits the presidential tenure to two terms. (1951)

Amendment XXIII

This amendment permits the residents of the District of Columbia to vote in elections for both the President and Vice President. (1961)

Amendment XXIV

The twenty-fourth amendment outlaws the Poll Tax in all federal elections and primaries. (1964)

Amendment XXV

Number 25 outlined procedures to fill vacancies in the Vice Presidency, and further clarifies the rules of presidential succession. (1967)

Amendment XXVI

The last amendment to be passed lowers the voting age in federal and state elections to 18. (1971)

THE GETTYSBURG ADDRESS

One of the most quoted speeches of all time, The Gettysburg Address was given by President Abraham Lincoln on November 19, 1863, at the dedication of the Civil War Cemetery at Gettysburg, PA.

The Gettysburg Address

Fourscore and seven years ago our fathers brought forth, on this continent, a new nation, conceived in Liberty, and dedicated to the proposition that all men are created equal.

Now we are engaged in a great civil war, testing whether that nation, or any nation so conceived, and so dedicated, can long endure. We are met on a great battlefield of that war. We have come to dedicate a portion of that field, as a final resting-place for those who here gave their lives, that that nation might live. It is altogether fitting and proper that we should do this.

But, in a larger sense, we can not dedicate—we can not consecrate—we can not hallow—this ground. The brave men, living and dead, who struggled here, have consecrated it far above our poor power to add or detract. The world will little note, nor long remember what we say here, but it can never forget what they did here. It is for us the living, rather, to be dedicated here to the unfinished work which they who fought here have thus far so nobly advanced. It is rather for us to be here dedicated to the great task remaining before us—

that from these honored dead we take increased devotion to that cause for which they here gave the last full measure of devotion—that we here highly resolve that these dead shall not have died in vain—that this nation, under God, shall have a new birth of freedom—and that government of the people, by the people, for the people, shall not perish from the earth.

ABRAHAM LINCOLN, November 19, 1863

THE EMANCIPATION PROCLAMATION

While it did not free all slaves in the United States, President Lincoln's order abolished slavery in the Confederacy, by declaring free all persons held as slaves within any state or part of a state then in armed rebellion. An additional purpose of the Emancipation Proclamation was to deplete Southern manpower while enhancing support for the Union cause in the eyes of the world's leaders.

The Emancipation Proclamation

BY THE PRESIDENT OF THE UNITED STATES OF AMERICA: A PROCLAMATION

Whereas, on the twenty-second day of September, in the year of our Lord one thousand eight hundred and sixty-two, a proclamation was issued by the President of the United States, containing, among other things, the following, to wit:

That on the first day of January, in the year of our Lord one thousand eight hundred and sixty-three, all persons held as slaves within any State or designated part of a State, the people whereof shall then be in rebellion against the United States, shall be then, thenceforward, and forever free; and the Executive Government of the United States, including the military and naval authority there of, will recognize and maintain the freedom of such persons, and will do no act or acts to repress such persons, or any of them, in any efforts they may make for their actual freedom.

That the Executive will, on the first day of January aforesaid, by proclamation, designate the States and parts of States, if any, in which the people thereof, shall on that day be, in good faith, represented in the Congress of the United States by members chosen thereto at elections wherein a majority of the qualified voters of such State shall have participated, shall in the absence of strong countervailing testimony, be deemed conclusive evidence that such State, and the people thereof, are not then in rebellion against the United States.

Now, therefore, I, Abraham Lincoln, President of the United States, by virtue of the power in me invested as Commander-in-Chief, of the Army and Navy of the United States in time of actual armed rebellion against authority and government of the United States, and as a fit and necessary war measure for suppressing said rebellion, do, on this first day of January, in the year of our Lord one thousand eight hundred and sixty three, and in accordance with my purpose so to do publicly proclaimed for the full period of one hundred days, from the day first above mentioned, order and designate as the States and parts of States wherein the people thereof respectively, are this day in rebellion against their United States, the following to wit:

Arkansas, Texas, Louisiana, (except the Parishes of St. Bernard, Plaquemines, Jefferson, St. Johns,

St Charles, St. James, Ascension, Assumption, Terrebone, Lafourche, St. Mary, St. Martin, and Orleans, including the City of New Orleans), Mississippi, Alabama, Florida, Georgia, South Carolina, North Carolina, and Virginia (except the forty-eight counties designated as West Virginia, and also the counties of Berkley, Accomac, Northampton, Elizabeth-City, York, Princess Ann, and Norfolk, including the cities of Norfolk and Portsmouth, and which excepted parts are, for the present, left precisely as if this proclamation were not issued.

And by virtue of the power, and for the purpose aforesaid, I do order and declare that all persons held as slaves within said designated States, and parts of States, are, and henceforward shall be free; and the Executive government of the United States, including the military and naval authorities thereof, will recognize and maintain, the freedom of said persons.

And I hereby enjoin upon the people so declared to be free to abstain from all violence, unless in necessary self-defence; and I recommend to them that, in all cases when allowed, they labor faithfully for reasonable wages.

And I further declare and make known that such persons of suitable condition, will be received into the armed service of the United States to garrison forts, positions, stations, and other places, and to man vessels of all sorts in said service.

And upon this act, sincerely believed to be an act of justice, warranted by the Constitution, upon military necessity, I invoke the considerate judgment of mankind, and the gracious favor of Almighty God.

In witness whereof, I have hereunto set my hand and caused the seal of the United States to be affixed.

Done at the City of Washington, the first day of January, in the year of our Lord one thousand eight hundred and sixty three, and of the Independence of the United States of America the eighty-seventh.

By the President: ABRAHAM LINCOLN
WILLIAM H. SEWARD, Secretary of State.

IN GOD WE TRUST

The phrase, "In God We Trust," originated during the Civil War when Rev. M.R. Watkinson, of Ridleyville, Pa., concerned about the loss of Union morale after several defeats during the Civil War, wrote the following to the Secretary of the Treasury, Salmon P. Chase: "From my heart I have felt our national shame in disowning God as not the least of our present national disasters." He went on to suggest "recognition of the Almighty God in some form on our coins."

Secretary Chase responded by ordering designs to appear on all coinage which included the phrase "In God We Trust." The design and slogan first appeared in 1864, and went on to appear and disappear on U.S. coins until 1955, when Congress ordered the phrase to be place on all U.S. paper money and coinage. In 1956, Congress designated "In God We Trust" as the official U.S. National Motto.

THE
UNITED STATES
FLAG

John Cabot raised the first flag—with the banners of England and St. Mark—in the United States in 1497. Gradually, each and every territory flew its own flag, and by 1707, each colony had its own unique flag, similar to the state flags of today.

The first flag to represent all of the colonies was flown on Prospect Hill in Boston at the Battle of Bunker Hill. The "Grand Union" flag contained the red cross of St. George and the white cross of St. Andrew combined in the blue canton, as well as 13 alternating red and white horizontal stripes.

In 1777, the Continental Congress adopted the following resolution: "Resolved: that the flag of the United States be thirteen stripes, alternate red and white; that the Union be thirteen stars, white on a blue field, representing a new constellation." Francis Hopkinson, designer of the naval flag, claimed to have designed this flag, although some believe that Betsy Ross made the first Stars and Stripes. William Driver, a sea captain, is said to have created the nickname. "Old Glory."

Two stripes and two stars were added in 1794 to represent the new states of Vermont and Kentucky, and it is at this time that the nickname "The Star-Spangled Banner" was used. In 1818, Congress voted to keep the number of stripes at 13, but to add a star to the field for each new state that was admitted.

The 50 star flag of the U.S. was officially raised for the first time on July 4, 1960 at Fort McHenry National Monument in Baltimore, MD.

The Pledge of Allegiance

"I pledge allegiance to the flag of the United States of America, and to the Republic for which it stands, one nation under God, indivisible, with liberty and justice for all."

Francis Bellamy wrote the pledge in 1892. The phase "under God" was added to the pledge by a 1954 act of Congress. Additionally, the original phrase "my flag" was changed to "flag of the United States of America."

THE STAR-SPANGLED BANNER

Designated as the National Anthem by Congress on March 3, 1931, "The Star-Spangled Banner" was written by Washington D.C. lawyer, Francis Scott Key, as he witnessed the September, 1814 shelling of Fort McHenry by British troops. The fort survived the assault, and the sight of the American flag at dawn (now displayed at the Smithsonian Institution) so inspired Key, that he immediately wrote out several verses. Key's brother-in-law, Judge J.H. Nicholson, suggested the tune for the song. It is interesting to note that Key's phrase "In God is our trust!" is the early forerunner to the United States National Motto, "In God We Trust."

The Star-Spangled Banner

I

Oh, say can you see by the dawn's early light
   What so proudly we hailed at the twilight's last gleaming?
Whose broad stripes and bright stars thru the peilous fight,
   O'er the ramparts we watched were so gallantly streaming?
And the rocket's red glare, the bombs bursting in air,
   Gave proof through the night that our flag was still there.
Oh, say does that star-spangled banner yet wave
   O'er the land of the free and the home of the brave?

II

On the shore, dimly seen through the mists of the
  deep,
  Where the foe's haughty host in dread silence
    reposes,
What is that which the breeze, o'er the towering
  steep,
  As it fitfully blows, half conceals, half discloses?
Now it catches the gleam of the morning's first
  beam,
  In full glory reflected no whines in the stream:
'Tis the star-spangled banner! Oh long may it wave
  O'er the land of the free and the home of the
    brave!

III

And where is that band who so vauntingly swore
  That the havoc of war and the battle's confusion,
A home and a country should leave us no more!
  Their blood has washed out their foul footstep's
    pollution.
No refuge could save the hireling and slave
  From the terror of flight, or the gloom of the grave:
And the star-spangled banner in triumph doth wave
  O'er the land of the free and the home of the
    brave!

IV

Oh! thus be it ever, when freemen shall stand
  Between their loved home and the war's
    desolation!

Blest with victory and peace, may the heav'n
  rescued land
  Praise the Power that hath made and preserved
  us a nation.
Then conquer we must, when our cause it is just,
  And this be our motto: "In God is our trust."
And the star-spangled banner in triumph shall
  wave
O'er the land of the free and the home of the
  brave!

THE STATUE OF LIBERTY

Designed by Frederic Auguste Bartholdi, the Statue of Liberty was given to the United States by the Franco-American Union of the American Revolution. The statue was completed on May 21, 1884, and arrived, dismantled, in over 200 packing cases, in June 1885. It was formally dedicated by President Grover Cleveland on October 28, 1886, and became a national monument in 1924.

The following sonnet by Emma Lazarus is engraved on the statue's pedestal:

The New Colossus
Not like the brazen giant of greek fame,
With conquering limbs astride from land to land;
Here at our sea-washed, sunset gates shall stand
A mighty woman with a torch, whose flame
Is the imprisoned lightning, and her name
Mother of Exiles. From her beacon-hand
Glows world-wide welcome; her mild eyes command
The air-bridged harbor that twin cities frame.
"Keep ancient lands, your storied pomp!" cries she
With silent lips. "Give me your tired, your poor,
Your huddled masses yearning to breathe free,
The wretched refuse of your teeming shore.
Send these, the homeless, tempest-tost to me.
I lift my lamp beside the golden door!"

Facts About the Statue of Liberty

Height from base to torch—151 feet, 1 inch.

Height from foundation of pedestal to torch—305 feet, 1 inch.

Height from heel to top of head—111 feet, 1 inch.

Height from the chin to cranium—17 feet, 3 inches.

Length of right arm—42 feet.

Length of tablet—23 feet, 7 inches.

Length of nose—4 feet, 6 inches.

Length of hand—16 feet, 5 inches.

Length of index finger—8 feet.

Thickness of waist—35 feet.

Thickness of head from ear to ear—10 feet.

Thickness of tablet—2 feet.

Thickness of right arm—12 feet.

Weight—450,000 pounds.

Width of mouth—3 feet.

Width of tablet—13 feet, 7 inches.

Number of stairs—167 from the land level to the top of the pedestal, 168 inside the head of the statue, and 54 rungs on the ladder leading to the arm holding the torch.

Circumference at second joint—3 feet, 6 inches.

Size of finger nail—13 inches by 10 inches.

Distance across the eye—2 feet, 6 inches.

NOTES

NOTES

NOTES

NOTES